STEP 4 Our friendly ghost has arms to greet you with! Make curves pointing toward the center of the body, with slight indents along the top so it looks like it has hands.

STEP 5 Draw a heart over the hands.

STEP 6 Add another heart next to the ghost.

STEP 7 Draw one more heart on the other side—or as many as you want!

STEP 8

Finish your hearts and draw circles or ovals toward the top center of the eyes to be the whites of the eyes. Color the rest of the eyes black. Add color to the hearts, blush to the ghost's cheeks, and shadows to the body as you like.

DRAWING SPOOKY CHIBI

LEARN HOW TO DRAW
Kawaii Vampires, Zombies, Ghosts, Skeletons, Monsters, and Other Cute, Creepy, and Gothic Creatures

Illustrations by Tessa Creative Art
Text by Sarah E. White

BLOOM BOOKS
FOR YOUNG READERS

Published by:
Bloom Books for Young Readers,
an imprint of Ulysses Press
PO Box 3440
Berkeley, CA 94703
www.ulyssespress.com

ISBN: 978-1-64604-496-2
Library of Congress Control Number: 2023932430

Printed in the United States by Versa Press
10 9 8 7 6 5 4 3

Acquisitions editor: Kierra Sondereker
Managing editor: Claire Chun
Editor: Renee Rutledge
Proofreader: Hanna Richards
Front cover design and illustrations: Fiverr
Layout: Winnie Liu

CONTENTS

THE
UNDEAD

GHOST

Ghosts can be spooky, or scary, or cute, and this classic haunt is definitely in the last category! It's also really easy to draw, so this is a great place to start if you're new to drawing chibis—or drawing in general.

STEP 1   Start the ghost with a rounded top that curves inward at the middle of the right side. Draw a wavy line at the bottom and a straight line along the left side.

STEP 2   For the eyes, draw large ovals tilted slightly toward the center in the middle of the ghost's circular face.

STEP 3   Draw a mouth between the eyes. It should look like a circle with a dip in the top, or an upturned macaroni noodle.

Keep going from step 1.

Try a few from scratch.

SKELETON

This sweet skeleton doesn't want to haunt, she wants to hug. This version wears a bow, but feel free to add a witch's hat or other embellishments as you like.

STEP 1   Start with the skull. Draw a circle almost all the way around, but at the bottom add three short, curved lines to make the chin area of the skull.

STEP 2   Draw large ovals for the eye holes toward the bottom of the skull, tilting toward center. Add a small triangular nose hole between them.

STEP 3   Make this skeleton's large bow by drawing two heart shapes touching at their bases, with a circle on top of the center point. Add a couple of lines to look like folds in the bow.

STEP 4 Next, sketch in the rib cage and spine. Start with a U shape for the base of the skull, then add two sets of parallel lines perpendicular to that shape for the shoulders. Draw two parallel lines running down the center of the drawing for the spine, and three sets of ribs on each side. Then add one longer bone that goes all the way across the waist.

STEP 5 Add the arm bones on the right side of the drawing. The upper arm is a longer rectangle, with an almost square joint for the lower arm, a curved line for the hand, and five straight fingers.

STEP 6 Repeat on the left side of the drawing for the second arm.

STEP 7

Now it's time for leg bones! The leg on the right side is bent back, so it starts with a U next to the ribs, with two squarish joints behind that. Add an oval for the foot and four square toes.

STEP 8

The leg on the left side is straight, drawn with two squares coming down at a slight diagonal from the chest. The foot is turned out, with the same square toes. Add shadows and eye shine to the eyes and color in the nose hole. Add other color as you like.

Keep going from step 1.

Try a few from scratch.

Zombies are generally not very cute, which makes sense, since they're undead. The chibi version drools and is a little short on brains, but it makes up for this by being weirdly cute.

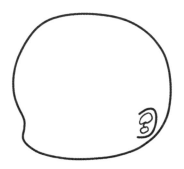

STEP 1 Draw a circular shape for the zombie's head, with a little dent at the lower left side. Draw a sideways U at the lower right of the drawing for the zombie's ear. Include a couple of rough circles attached by a line inside the ear shape.

STEP 2 Draw an oval close to the lower left edge to make an eye. Sketch an eyelid that looks like a hat across the top third of that eye, then make a heavy black circle underneath. The right eye is an egg-shaped black hole. Top both eyes with thick sideways S-shaped eyebrows.

STEP 3 Sketch tufts of hair at the top and sides of the head. Add a wavy line with short, straight lines intersecting it to show where the zombie's head has been sewn back together.

STEP 4

Make a mouth along the bottom of the head, between the eyes. It should look like half a rectangle with curved corners. Add a couple of square teeth at the center. Include a tiny C shape between the eyes for its nose.

STEP 5

Start to build the zombie's shirt by drawing a rough square below the head. The bottom edge should be wavy. Add a couple of triangular shapes at the top right and a patched rectangle at the bottom right of the body.

STEP 6

Draw sleeves. The left sleeve starts with a large oval right below the face, connected to the body with an almost straight line. On the right side, draw the sleeve on top of the shirt with an oval, two parallel lines behind it, and a line connecting them at the top right of the shirt.

STEP 7

Add long-fingered hands that partially overlap the sleeves. Sketch in baggy patched-up pants below the shirt.

STEP 8

Finally, draw the zombie's shoes. They should be rounded at the front and mostly flat along the bottom, with a straight line at the back connecting them to the pants. Erase any guidelines or places where you drew over other details. Color in as you like, and don't forget some drool!

THE UNDEAD

Keep going from step 1.

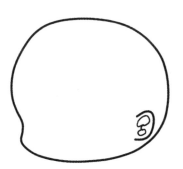

Try a few from scratch.

VAMPIRE

Vampires are classic creatures of the night, known to fly around and suck people's blood. This version looks pretty harmless with his tiny teeth and little wings, but it sure is fun to draw!

STEP 1

Start with an almost straight line for the bottom of the face. Curve in the sides of the face where the ears attach, near the bottom on each side. For the top of the head, draw a wide V shape. Add pointy leaf shapes for ears, mimicking the same shape on the inside of the ear.

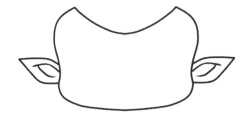

STEP 2

Our vampire's hair looks like a helmet with bat ears. Start on one side above the ear and draw a line going up, with a little dent in it toward the top. Add a pointed shape at the top and a long curve above the head. Repeat the same shape in the opposite direction on the other side of the head.

STEP 3

Next, draw large, almond-shaped eyes, one on each side of the face. Have them point down toward the center of the face. Below and between the eyes, add a straight line with a U shape connecting underneath for the mouth. Don't forget two tiny triangular fangs!

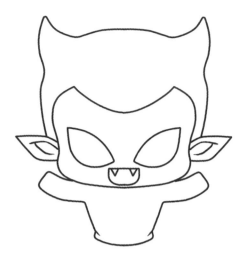

STEP 4

Sketch a curved line that follows the bottom of the face and extends out below the ears. Add narrow rectangles for the sleeves and lines that slant inward slightly to form the sides of the body. Add a curved line to connect these two lines for the bottom of the jacket.

STEP 5

Make mitten shapes at the end of each sleeve. Add a V shape on the coat, with lines that start as wide as the vampire's mouth. Include vertical zigzags on each side of those lines, and two intersecting triangles between to make a bow tie. Add a circle below this for the jacket button.

STEP 6

Now it's time for legs. The left leg is a long rectangle, with a sort of wobbly U shape for the foot. The right leg is behind the left, so make a curved line for the top of the leg that intersects the left leg and add another little curve for the foot.

STEP 7

Draw large curves that come to points around the vampire's body, starting at the top of each ear and working your way around to the waist. These are the wings.

STEP 8

Outline segments of the wings, following the shapes you just drew. Color in the details as you like.

DRAWING SPOOKY CHIBI

Keep going from step 1.

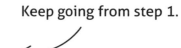

Try a few from scratch.

MUMMY

A mummy isn't spooky in its original form, but some mummies wake up to become monsters in the vein of zombies or skeletons. Our version is super cute and gives you lots of practice drawing curved lines for the bandages!

STEP 1 Draw the top of the mummy's head as you would the top of a circle, with indentations on the sides at the bottom. For the bottom of the face, draw a wobbly, slightly curved line.

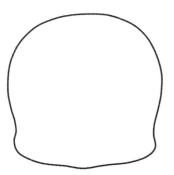

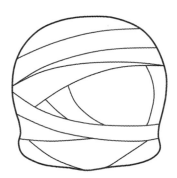

STEP 2 Sketch the rough lines of a face inside the shape you just drew: a wide V at the bottom and a curve along the right side. Leave space for an eye on the right side and space for a mouth within the V. Then cover the rest of the face with gently curved sets of parallel lines for bandages.

STEP 3 Add most of a circle (partially covered by a bandage) in the empty space for the mummy's eye, then fill it in with black. Draw a thick curve over the eye.

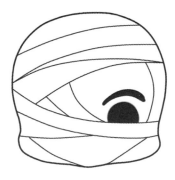

STEP 4

Next, add a mouth in the space at the bottom of the head. Draw a U shape that's slightly taller on one side, then a line connecting the top of each side. Add another line below that inside the mouth. Draw a shorter curved line above the eye for the eyebrow.

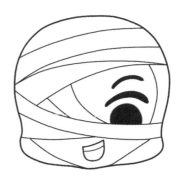

STEP 5

Draw the mummy's torso as a large U shape that gets a little narrower at the top. Cover this shape with lines to indicate wraps on the body.

STEP 6

Draw short arms by making narrow U shapes. Add lines for wraps and curved lines that follow the lines of a wrap on each arm to make it look like the bandages are unraveling.

STEP 7

Add legs. The left leg should be an oval overlapping the bottom third of the body. The right leg should be another short U shape below the body.

STEP 8

Add wraps to the legs in the same way you did the rest of the body. Add details to the eye and color in as desired.

Keep going from step 1.

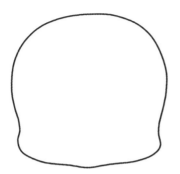

Try a few from scratch.

BRIDE OF FRANKENSTEIN

If the monster in the Frankenstein story is actually Frankenstein's Monster, shouldn't the Bride of Frankenstein actually be the Bride of Frankenstein's Monster? Whatever you call her, this character originated in the 1935 movie *Bride of Frankenstein* and is almost as popular as the original creation (who you'll find in chibi form on page 33).

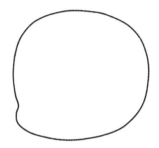

STEP 1
Draw a large circle with a small indentation at the lower left side of our Bride's face.

STEP 2
Add ovals for eyes, with the left eye close to the side of the face and the right one just off center. Sketch in arches above the ovals and small tear-shaped eyebrows.

STEP 3
Sketch a scalloped line above the eyebrows to start the Bride's hair. Leave an ear shape toward the bottom right side of the face. Add a line with larger curves above the head for the hair piled on top. Draw a small C for her nose below the eyes and a curve below that for the mouth. Don't forget two little triangular teeth!

STEP 4

Add wavy horizontal lines in a few places through the hair. Draw shapes in the ear space to make it look more like an ear. Add short lines for a neck and connect them with a curved line.

STEP 5

Draw a line below the hairline and add vertical lines for stitches. Add a bolt to the right side of the head (it's a square with a circle on top), then add another line that follows the curve and part of a bolt on the left side. Add a rough square around the neck for the torso.

STEP 6

The Bride's skirt comes next. Add diagonal lines starting at the waist like the sides of an A. Make the bottom edge wavy. Add a curved line at the waist and a triangle and rectangle overlapping on one side behind the skirt to make a tie.

STEP 7

Draw a rectangle going toward the center from the right shoulder, and add fingers. The left-side arm runs alongside the body with the hand under the right hand. Add teardrop-shaped tiers on top of the shoulders to make little sleeves for the dress, and partial ovals for her feet.

STEP 8

Add details to the eyes. Erase any overlapping areas or guidelines. Color as you want.

THE UNDEAD

Keep going from step 1.

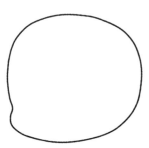

Try a few from scratch.

FRANKENSTEIN'S MONSTER

Now that we know how to draw the Bride of Frankenstein, let's finish off the ghastly couple with a lesson on Frankenstein's Monster. He's actually looking pretty dapper in his suit and lab-coat-length jacket. He must be getting ready for the wedding!

STEP 1   Start with a large circle for his head, with a little indentation at the lower right side of the drawing.

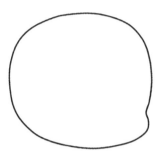

STEP 2   Sketch large ovals for eyes. The right eye is close to the right side of the head, while the left is just a little left of center. Add arches above the eyes and tear-shaped eyebrows above those.

STEP 3   Add a backward C shape low between the eyes for the nose and a curve below that for his smile. Add two little triangular teeth. Sketch in chunky hair around and above the head, leaving an ear shape toward the lower left side of the face. Add shapes to the ear to give it depth.

STEP 4

Draw a straight line running down from the head on the left side of the body, with a curve along the bottom and a slight curve back up on the right side. This body shape should be centered on about the center third of the head. Draw bolts on each side of the head—they're made with short rectangles with circles on top—and a curved vertical line below the hairline with short vertical lines for stitches.

STEP 5

Draw our monster's arms close to the body, bent at the elbows, with the hands lifted to the center of the chest and closed in fists.

STEP 6

Add a V shape at the center of the body and draw a vertical line down the center. Draw triangles between the hands and the head, and lines on each side coming down from the triangles' edges below the hands and body to make the coat. There's more of the coat visible on the left side of the drawing, but the shapes are rectangular on both sides.

DRAWING SPOOKY CHIBI

STEP 7

Next, add a bow tie just below the V by drawing two triangles with their points facing each other, and a circle on top. Add rectangles below the torso and behind the coat for pant legs, with a small, curved line connecting them and another line at the waist to make a waistband on the pants. Finally, add feet.

STEP 8

Add details to the eyes. Erase any guidelines or lines that overlap. Color in your monster.

DRAWING SPOOKY CHIBI

Keep going from step 1.

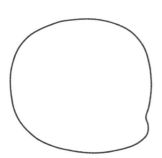

Try a few from scratch.

THE UNDEAD

ONRYŌ

In Japanese folklore, onryō are ghosts, usually considered vengeful and able to cause harm to people in the world of the living. This cute version with a dress on looks like a ghost, but a generally sweet one.

STEP 1 Start with a curve for the top of the head. Draw the sides of the head somewhat straight, with indentations close to the bottom on each side and a slightly curved line along the bottom.

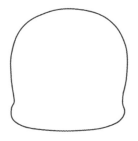

STEP 2 Sketch the beginning of the onryō's hair by drawing long bangs that cover where her eye would go on the left side of the face. The hair on the right side is brushed back but the same length.

STEP 3 Add a large oval eye in the space left on the right side of the face. Draw a heavy arch over the eye and a teardrop-shaped eyebrow above that. Sketch a smile at the center of the face toward the bottom.

STEP 4

Draw the neck next. It starts with two parallel lines attached to the bottom center of the head, curving out slightly. The top of the dress is drawn with a V-shaped neckline that flattens out toward the shoulders. The sides and bottom form a gently curved square.

STEP 5

Add the bottom of the dress by drawing a flared skirt. The lines start somewhat straight on each side then flare out toward the bottom. Make a ragged line for the bottom of the skirt.

STEP 6

Next, draw in long, flowing sleeves on each side of the top of the dress. Only the onryō's little hands should peek out from the ends.

STEP 7

Starting above the top of the head, sketch long, wavy lines almost as long as the dress for the onryō's hair. Add waves behind her body. Draw a bow at the center-front waist of the dress by making two blocky heart shapes with their tips touching and a circle on top. Add rectangles hanging down for the ties of the bow.

STEP 8

Add details to the eye. Erase any guidelines or overlapping areas. Color in as desired.

THE UNDEAD

Keep going from step 1.

Try a few from scratch.

HEADLESS HORSEMAN

The Headless Horseman is a Halloween legend of a man with no head riding around the countryside on his horse, trying to find a replacement head. This version skips the gore (though you can see an empty neck in the background) and would make a pretty cute Halloween drawing.

STEP 1 Start with the horse's head, making it oval in shape but wider at the top than the bottom. The head should be close to the left edge of your paper.

STEP 2 Sketch in hair on top of the horse's head. It should have rough, spiky edges. Add a small triangle at the left side of the head for part of one ear and a larger, leaf-shaped ear on the right side. Draw a line a little back from center to give the ear dimension. Add small ovals for eyes, smaller circles for nostrils, and a little curved smile.

STEP 3 Draw a large oval, slightly overlapping the horse's face, for the body. Sketch in a mane flowing from the back of the head to the top of the oval.

STEP 4

Add four legs. The horse is galloping, so the front legs should be longer, curved, and raised, while the back legs should be shorter and curved. Add a short, S-shaped tail with a leaf shape at the end.

STEP 5

Above the horse and to the right, begin to draw the pumpkin head. It starts with an oval shape at the center, with a couple of curved lines connecting to it on each side to make a pumpkin shape.

DRAWING SPOOKY CHIBI

STEP 6 Give the pumpkin a short stem and a scary face. We went with slanted rectangles for eyes and a classic zigzag mouth.

STEP 7 Our horse needs a rider! Start with the fingers curled up around the bottom of the pumpkin to hold it. From there, add a circular shape for the arm. Behind the pumpkin, a half circle and a short line make the horseman's neck. Sketch in a flowing cloak with little triangular collars and a circle clasp.

STEP 8

How does a headless horseman harvest a new head? With a really big knife, of course! Behind the horse's head, add part of a rectangle for the sleeve and a hand with oval fingers gripping the rectangular handle of the knife. Curve the blade along the top edge, making a smaller curve along the bottom. Connect them with an almost straight line. Add another line along the bottom of the blade to give it a little depth. Draw a rectangle behind the horse's mane for our rider's leg, and add a little shoe. Erase any lines where shapes overlap, and color as you like.

DRAWING SPOOKY CHIBI

Keep going from step 1.

Try a few from scratch.

BANSHEE

In Irish folklore, banshees are spirits that herald an upcoming death, usually by screaming or making some other unpleasant noise. While our chibi version doesn't scream, she's still a little spooky and will give you lots of practice drawing wild hair.

STEP 1 Draw the top of the banshee's head to be circular, with a bottom edge that curves out a bit along the bottom.

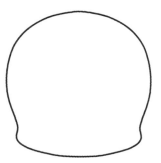

STEP 2 Draw almond-shaped eyes pointing down and inward close to the bottom of the head.

STEP 3 Add a triangular nose below and between the eyes. Begin to sketch the hair with chunky bangs that cover the forehead.

STEP 4   Draw a short square torso underneath the head.

STEP 5   Add short, chunky arms raised up behind the head. Sketch the shirt, flaring it out at the sides and giving it a similar ragged edge like the banshee's hair.

STEP 6   Draw a wavy line at the end of each arm and long, rectangular fingers pointed down. Add short, skinny legs lined up with the torso.

STEP 7 Have fun giving your banshee a lot of hair! Draw lots of chunky points all around the banshee's body, almost as long as she is tall and radiating all around. Also add sleeves covering most of the arm and hanging down in a triangular shape below the arm.

STEP 8 Add short diagonal lines to the sleeves. Draw a waistband at the bottom of the torso, and double lines in a backward Y shape along the body to make the top of the dress. Add more lines to show folds in the fabric. Erase any overlapping or extra lines and color in.

THE UNDEAD

Keep going from step 1.

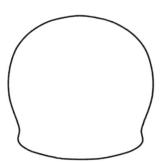

Try a few from scratch.

DRAWING SPOOKY CHIBI

THE SUPERNATURAL

WITCH

This little witch is anything but wicked! With a frilly dress and flowing hair, she's lots of fun to draw. It's up to you to decide if she's carrying tricks or treats to the spooky party!

STEP 1 Start with the back of the witch's head, drawing a curve that flattens into a straight line on the right side of the face. Make the line jut out a bit for the chin then gently curve back around, with a small oval jutting out at the bottom left for the ear. Include a little squared-off circle in the inner ear and a smaller circle for the earlobe.

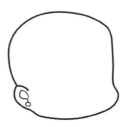

STEP 2 Draw large, round, black eyes lining up with the ear on each side of the face. Add a thick curved-down line at the top of each eye and another a little above each eye. Make a tiny sideways V between the eyes for her nose.

STEP 3 Add a U shape with a line on top below the nose for the witch's mouth. Begin to sketch in hair by starting with a curve that follows the top of the head shape then turns into waves behind the head. Add wavy lines behind the head and on the right side of the face. Sketch in slightly curved triangles across the forehead for bangs.

STEP 4   Draw a witch hat on top of the head. Start with a long, curved line that goes around the head, then add a shorter line that follows the same curve to make the brim of the hat. Sketch lines coming up from the curve as if you were going to draw a triangle, then make the tip point back to the left. Add another line above the other curves for the hat band.

STEP 5   Add a crescent moon to the front of the hat. Draw short parallel lines below the center of the face for a neck, and perpendicular lines attached to these for the shoulders. Make a curve for the neckline of the dress, a lazy, backward S on the right side for the front of the dress, and ruffled sleeves.

STEP 6

Draw short arms coming out of the sleeves to hold the broom. On the witch's right hand (or her left side as she's facing you) you should see all of her fingers; on her left hand, make only her thumb visible. Sketch in a wavy line most of the way around her body for the bottom of the dress, then add lines going up toward the waist to enhance the folds and ruffles. Draw in parallel lines for the broom (leaving a small gap that the handle of the bag will cover) with a circle joining them at the front, and curved lines at the back.

STEP 7

Start the bristles of the broom by drawing a large V on its side with the base intersecting the end of the handle. Draw a wavy line at the open end between the two lines, then add in some lines to make bristles. Sketch in curled boots under the center front of the skirt and add a round bag cinched at the top, hanging from the top of the handle.

DRAWING SPOOKY CHIBI

STEP 8

Add details to the eyes: black circles at the center and a bit of eye shine. Draw a skull on the bag consisting of a circle with a line of little squares along the bottom edge. Add large ovals for its eyeholes, and a little nose hole. Erase any lines that overlap. Color as you like to add blush to the cheeks, highlights to the hair, and so on.

Keep going from step 1.

Try a few from scratch.

DRAWING SPOOKY CHIBI

WIZARD

Wizards can be good or evil, but this little wizard definitely sides with good. As drawing people goes, this is pretty simple because of the cloak that covers more of their body. Add any shape you like to the end of the wizard's wand, or add different designs to the cloak.

STEP 1 Start with a large circle for the head. There should be a little dent at the lower left side and a curve extending out a bit from the lower right side for an ear. Add shapes inside that shape for the inside of the ear.

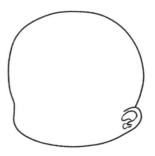

STEP 2 Draw large dark ovals for eyes in the bottom third of the face. Add curved lines above them that touch the eye, and another, thicker set above the eyes.

STEP 3 Add a small C shape between the eyes for the nose. Below that, draw a larger curve slanted toward the right side of the drawing for the mouth. Starting around the ear, sketch in chunky hair and bangs with pointed tips. Draw a curve that follows the top of the head for the cloak's hood.

STEP 4

Continue sketching the hood. Draw a line that starts at the bottom center of the face, curves up around the side of the head higher than the one you just drew, and around the other side in the same manner. Add two parallel lines that go from the top left of the head around to the bottom right side to add dimension to the hood.

STEP 5

Draw a large, flowing shirt shape to make the body of the cloak. Start with a large L on the left side of the drawing, then add sleeves on either side. The left arm will be lifted to hold the wand, so that sleeve is shorter and more of a square, while the right-side sleeve points down in a rectangular shape.

STEP 6

Sketch a blocky hand below the sleeve on the right side and a column of rectangles near the left sleeve for that hand. Add a thumb in front of the fingers. Draw in short legs with curved feet, and crescent-shaped shoes with straps.

STEP 7

Draw parallel vertical lines above and below the hand for the wand, with a slightly curved line at the bottom. Add a large star on top, with a smaller star drawn inside the larger star and lines outlining the left sides and bottom to give it depth.

STEP 8

Add details to the cloak as you like. We included partial star shapes on the hood and circles and curves on the body. Add eye details and color in.

DRAWING SPOOKY CHIBI

Keep going from step 1.

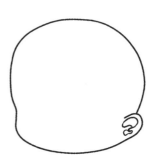

Try a few from scratch.

KILLER CLOWN

Clowns are rather controversial characters. Some people love them and find them funny. Others think they are creepy, set to turn on you at any moment. This cute "killer" clown has a little bit of both aspects, juggling for cheers while its face drips blood.

STEP 1   Draw the basic shape of the clown's head as a rough square with a rounded top and slight indents on the sides toward the bottom.

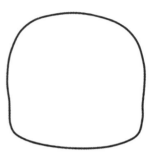

STEP 2   Sketch diamonds low on the face with large ovals on top of them. Fill in the ovals. Add curves that touch the tops of the oval and follow the lines of the diamond. Draw sideways tear shapes above the points of the diamonds.

STEP 3   Place a small C low between the eyes. Draw a sausage shape below the nose, with a smaller shape inside. Add vertical lines for teeth.

STEP 4

Add puffy clouds of hair all around the head. The top of the head should be covered with one large shape, with smaller shapes going down the sides of the head.

STEP 5

Sketch a slightly flattened circle for the clown's body, with the top of the circle narrowing into the clown's neck.

STEP 6

Our clown is a juggler, so draw arms raised and hands with blocky fingers pointing upward as if throwing and catching balls. Add short rectangles for the legs and little oval-like shapes for the shoes.

STEP 7
Draw two hearts on their sides, connected at their bases with a circle to make a bow tie directly under the clown's mouth. From the center of the tie, draw two gently curved lines that meet at the bottom of the body. Add two circles for buttons. Sketch a slightly curved horizontal line just below center on the body, then add vertical lines to the lower section.

STEP 8
Add five (or however many you like) circles around the clown's head. Add details to the eyes. Erase any overlapping lines or guidelines, and color in as you like. Don't forget to add a little gore if you want!

THE SUPERNATURAL

Keep going from step 1.

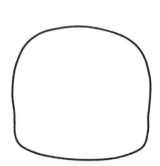

Try a few from scratch.

DRAWING SPOOKY CHIBI

BLACK CAT

Black cats have a bad reputation for hanging out with witches, demons, and other scary folk. As the owner of a black cat, I can tell you they aren't any more evil or mischievous than any other kinds of cats. Of course, they're cats, so that's not saying much. This kitty is definitely cute, though, no matter what color you make it.

STEP 1   Start drawing the cat's head on the upper left-side of your paper. The bottom of the head should gently curve, while the sides should indent slightly at the bottom then get slightly narrower as they go up to the triangular ears. Connect them with a straight line at the base of the ears.

STEP 2   Draw large black circles toward the bottom of the face, with arches over the top touching the circles.

STEP 3   Between the eyes, draw a circle with a pointed bottom to be the cat's nose. Shape the eyebrows like teardrops on their sides.

STEP 4   Sketch two short curves under the nose and add a triangular shape to the right ear.

STEP 5   Add a large oval shape starting in line with the center of the left eye and going out behind the head to make the cat's body. Draw short lines for whiskers.

STEP 6   Start drawing the back leg with a C-shape that goes down past the edge of the body, ending in a stubby little leg. Add two legs around the middle of the body and one more, slightly bent, at the front of the body, as if the cat is walking.

STEP 7   Give your cat a fat tail raised behind the cat in a question mark shape. This means your cat is ready to play!

STEP 8

Draw a circle with a star in it below the center of the face. Add details to the eyes. Erase any extra lines or places where lines overlap. Color as desired.

Keep going from step 1.

Try a few from scratch.

BAT

Bats are often associated with vampires and other creatures of the night, but in reality, bats are really cool creatures that literally eat tons of insects. This bat looks a little bit like a cat with wings. It's very cute and easy to draw.

STEP 1 Sketch out the head of the bat. Draw a shape like a lemon, with pointed ends on the sides and triangular ear shapes on top. Draw a short horizontal line at the center top of the head, below the ears.

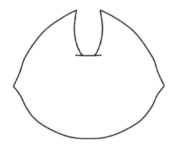

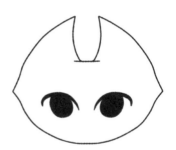

STEP 2 Add black oval eyes with arches above, just touching the ovals at the top. They should be centered vertically on the head but low down on the face.

STEP 3 Make teardrop-shaped eyebrows above the eyes. Add a small circular nose that comes to a point at the bottom, with two curves below it and an oval tongue sticking out below. Add lines to the ears to make a sort of almond shape at the outside of the ears.

STEP 4 Sketch a V shape that's curved back toward the body, with rough edges to make a tuft of fur below the head.

STEP 5 Add a smaller shape in a similar contour below the first furry shape.

STEP 6 Draw three little oval toes on each side of the second tuft of fur for the bat's feet.

STEP 7 Sketch in bat wings. Starting next to the foot on each side, make sweeping scallops up and around to behind the head. Add another line and little fingers at the top of the wing on each side.

STEP 8 Draw lines to shape the contours of the wings. Add details to the eyes. Erase any extra lines and color in as you wish.

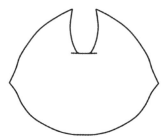

Keep going from step 1.

Try a few from scratch.

SPIDER

Some people are afraid of spiders, even though spiders are a key part of the natural world. Giant person-eating spiders are popular in fantasy and horror stories, and while this version has little pincers, the worst it could do is give you a tiny pinch.

STEP 1 Sketch the spider's body to look sort of like a pumpkin, with three curves along the bottom. Make the top taller at the center and with shorter, sharper curves.

STEP 2 Extend the lines on the bottom curve slightly, then draw large, teardrop-shaped eyes pointing inward in this center section.

STEP 3 Add eyebrows shaped like elbow macaroni.

STEP 4 Sketch in the pincers below the eyes.

THE SUPERNATURAL

STEP 5 Start adding legs at the bottom on each side. The first set is almost square, while the second set on each side is more heart shaped, with the tip of the heart behind the body.

STEP 6 Add two more sets of legs on each side. These also have the heart shape at the end but are more square close to the body.

STEP 7 Draw little curved ends on the bottom for two sets of feet. These lines should curve downward and in toward the body.

STEP 8 Repeat on the last two sets of legs. Add eye details. Erase any extra or overlapping lines. Color as you like.

Keep going from step 1.

Try a few from scratch.

SCARECROW

Whenever something is given human features, there's always a chance it will come to life and cause havoc wherever it goes. Our chibi version wouldn't get very far, given that it has no legs, but it's too cute to be terrifying anyway.

STEP 1 Draw a large circle for the head, with little V-shaped indentations close to the bottom on each side and a slightly curved line at the bottom.

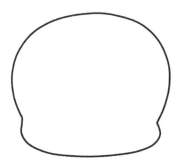

STEP 2 Sketch a long, narrow body that gets slightly wider at the base. Make the bottom line ragged.

STEP 3 Add large, dark oval eyes low on the face. Make a little curved line underneath each eye following the same curve.

STEP 4 Draw rectangular shapes going straight out from the body for the sleeves of its jacket. Add rectangular jacket fronts that come together a little below the top center edge of the torso.

STEP 5 Add a square shape coming out from the end of each sleeve, and sketch in parallel lines. Make a longer rectangular version at the bottom center. Draw teardrop-shaped eyebrows and a curve of a smile between the eyes, with short lines on top to look like stitching.

STEP 6 Sketch in the scarecrow's hat. Ours is flat on top with curved sides coming out to points at the sides of the head. Add horizontal lines toward the top of the head for a hat band.

STEP 7

Draw a large bow centered below the scarecrow's head. Start with a little rectangle at the center and candy corn–shaped triangles on each side. Add rectangles below to be the ends of the ribbon. Make jagged little lines coming out from the scarecrow's sleeves.

STEP 8

Add eye shine and any other details you would like to the eyes. Erase any overlapping lines or guidelines. Color in as desired.

DRAWING SPOOKY CHIBI

Keep going from step 1.

Try a few from scratch.

SCARY DOLL

Dolls, like clowns, can fall somewhere in the range from creepy to cute, fun to terrifying. This one leans a little toward the creepy side with its button eyes and stitched-on smile, though the ruffles and flowers tone it down a bit!

STEP 1 Draw a circle for the head that has an almost straight line instead of a curve on the doll's left side. There should be a little dent toward the bottom of that side as well.

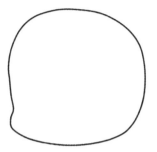

STEP 2 Add large circles with little curved lines following the curves inside the circle. Draw a little C shape below and between the circles for the nose.

STEP 3 Sketch in X shapes with dots at each end point to turn the circles into buttons. Add a curved line under the nose for the mouth, and short lines to make stitching. Draw in chunky, rectangular bangs, then add curved lines above and around the head to make hair. Add some additional lines at the bottom of the hair going up toward the face.

STEP 4 Draw thick arches over the button eyes. Add a squarish shape under the head for the torso. Sketch a flower in the doll's hair. Start at the center of the flower with a circle, then add petals around the circle, and more layers of petals underneath. Add leaf shapes on the sides.

STEP 5 On the right side of the body, add an upside-down U shape to form the top of the sleeve. Draw a ragged edge along the bottom, with a rectangular arm sticking out. Make the fingers straight, with a slight curve in the thumb and index finger. Add a smaller sleeve on the other side, and a short line coming out from the sleeve (this arm isn't really visible).

STEP 6 Sketch in a ruffled skirt. Draw a straight line in line with the bottom of the shirt, with a ruffled arc going across to behind the right arm, finishing with another line back to the waist. Add another layer of ruffles underneath.

STEP 7

Draw shoe shapes in front of the skirt. The shape is like the outside of an 8, with horizontal lines across the base of the shoe and an outline of the shape on the right-hand side of each shoe to add depth. Make a V shape at the top center of the shirt. Add curves below that to form the collar. Draw shapes that mimic the sleeve shapes at the center of the shirt to make a tie.

STEP 8

Erase areas where there are overlapping lines or guidelines. Color in as you like.

DRAWING SPOOKY CHIBI

Keep going from step 1.

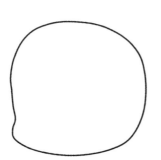

Try a few from scratch.

DRAWING SPOOKY CHIBI

THE MONSTROUS

CTHULHU

Cthulhu is an ancient creature of the deep, a combination of an octopus and a dragon. It doesn't sound very cute, but this chibi version is definitely more sweet than scary.

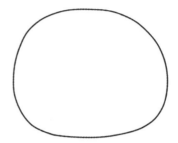

STEP 1 Start by drawing a slightly flattened large circle for the head.

STEP 2 Add two small ovals for the eyes, spaced wide apart and low on the head. They can be tilted in slightly. Color them black. Sketch in four short tentacles at the bottom of the head.

STEP 3 Draw a rounded rectangle below the tentacles for Cthulhu's body.

STEP 4 Sketch in short arms with zigzag lines to form three fingers on each hand.

STEP 5 Now add legs. The leg on the left side is taking a step. Draw it like a rectangle with a curve at the top and notches toward the bottom for the foot. The right-side leg should be mostly rectangular.

STEP 6 Add curved lines coming out from the back of the head and around the arms for the little monster's wings.

STEP 7

Sketch shapes in the wings that mimic the lines of the wings.

STEP 8

Add details to the eyes. Draw circles of different sizes to make spots across the head. Color in and add details.

THE MONSTROUS

Keep going from step 1.

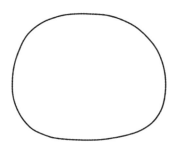

Try a few from scratch.

DRAWING SPOOKY CHIBI

WEREWOLF

Werewolves are cursed humans who turn into bloodthirsty, wolflike creatures under the influence of a full moon. The chibi version still has sharp teeth but doesn't look like it would hurt anyone.

STEP 1 Draw a rough oval for the werewolf's head, with an extra curve jutting out at the bottom and tufts of hair on the sides and top.

STEP 2 Sketch triangular shapes at the top of the head for the ears. Add black circles for the eyes, with thick arches above them and tear shapes above those.

STEP 3 Add a triangle between and just below the eyes for a nose, lining it up with the curve along the bottom of the face. Draw the inner ear on the werewolf's right-side ear, following the shape of the outside of the ear but with a wavy line across the bottom.

STEP 4

Draw lines from the center bottom of the nose curving up, then a U-shaped line below them to form the mouth. Add small rectangles or triangles for teeth. Sketch in a tuft of hair below the chin that comes to a point in line with the chin.

STEP 5

The rest of the werewolf's chest should be a rough square around that tuft of hair, with its own ragged lines for fur drawn in. Curve the left arm in as if the werewolf's hand were on its hip. Sketch in fur and draw a hand with short, curved fingers. On the werewolf's left side, draw the hand raised and the fingers as a line of overlapping ovals.

STEP 6

Draw two parallel and slightly curved lines to form the werewolf's belt. Add a rectangular buckle at the center and a skinny rectangle on each side for belt loops. Add the legs of its shorts by drawing rectangles with ragged bottom edges and a short line connecting them.

STEP 7 Add furry legs peeking out from under the shorts and large, blocky feet with four round toes on each foot.

STEP 8 Add details to the eyes. Color in the body, shorts, and other details.

DRAWING SPOOKY CHIBI

Keep going from step 1.

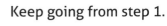

Try a few from scratch.

DEVIL

This little devil is so cute it's hard to believe it could ever be evil. The head is somewhat similar to that of a vampire, which helps you to see that the same elements, such as elf-like ears or horns, can be used to make a lot of different characters.

STEP 1   Draw a large circle with a dent at the bottom to make the devil's head.

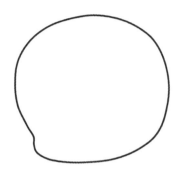

STEP 2   Sketch long, pointy ears low on the sides of the face (make the right-side ear bigger than the left). Follow the lines to make the same shapes smaller inside the ears, and add other curved lines for the inner ears. Draw large black eyes in line with the ears, curved lines pointing down for the outside of the eyes, and sideways S shapes arcing up over the eyes.

STEP 3   Add curved triangles connected to the head for the devil's horns. Again, the right is a little larger. Place a sideways U between the eyes for a nose, and a wide U shape tipped a little to the left with a line on top for the mouth. Add a curved horizontal line and two vertical lines inside the mouth.

STEP 4

Draw two short parallel lines from the center of the head, then connect them with a rounded rectangular body.

STEP 5

Sketch an arm in front of the body on the right side. The upper arm is oval shaped and almost as high as the bottom of the head. The lower arm is straight across the body, with rectangular fingers and a thumb pointing up. The left arm should have the same shape at the top, with a couple of fingers you can see below the right hand.

STEP 6

The upper right leg is a larger oval that crosses the devil's body completely so that the right lower leg is in front of the left leg on the left side of the body. Add a jagged line above the knee for the bottom of its shorts. The lower leg is straight to the curve of the ankle, with a wavy line for the toes. Draw the left leg behind the right leg; only the lower leg and foot should be visible.

STEP 7

Add the pitchfork. Behind the legs, draw part of a rectangle. To the left side of the body, follow those lines but make them come together in a point for the center of the fork. Draw a crescent shape pointing up and centered on the handle of the fork.

STEP 8

Draw a tail coming from the center back of the larger leg. Make two parallel lines in an S shape with a triangle at the end. Add details to the eyes and erase any overlapping lines or guidelines. Color in.

THE MONSTROUS

Keep going from step 1.

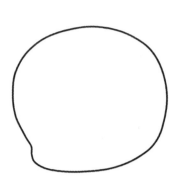

Try a few from scratch.

GRIM REAPER

This reaper isn't very grim, but it does have a very large scythe! The base of this one will be the same as the skeleton's but even easier to draw because of the cloak covering the body.

STEP 1   Start with a large circle, finishing it with three little curves at the bottom.

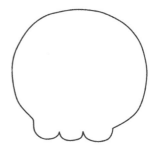

STEP 2   Add large ovals pointed slightly toward the center, and a small triangle below and between them.

STEP 3   Sketch a circular shape that follows the shape of the skull at the top but is wider than the skull along the sides at the bottom. Add another line starting at the center bottom, following the previous line along the left side of the face, then arching up over the head and ending in a point to form the top of the hood. On the reaper's right side, start at the center bottom of the face and draw a sort of backward L shape, curving up to make the other side of the hood.

STEP 4

The body of the cloak should be roughly centered on the skull. Draw lines that widen as they move away from the skull. Add a wavy line to the bottom that ends in a triangular point at the bottom right side of the drawing.

STEP 5

Add a rectangular shape along the right side of the body for the sleeve. The left arm is raised, so that sleeve is a shorter rectangle.

STEP 6

Draw in short, rectangular fingers just peeking out from the right-side sleeve. On the drawing's left side, the hand is curled around the scythe that will be there soon. Draw short lines for the hand connected by ovals for fingers.

STEP 7

Add the handle of the scythe by drawing two long parallel lines spaced as wide as the fingers are long. Add a little curved line to connect them at each end.

STEP 8

Finish off with the scythe blade, which runs behind the reaper's head. At the base of the blade, the blade begins as a rectangle, but on the other side of the head, it curves down to a triangular point. Erase any extra lines and add color.

Keep going from step 1.

Try a few from scratch.

DRAWING SPOOKY CHIBI

BAPHOMET

Baphomet is a goatlike creature originally associated with the Knights Templar, a former Catholic military order. These days Baphomet is usually portrayed as a demon. The chibi version looks a little like a cat with wings and horns.

STEP 1 Draw Baphomet with a squared-off jawline, so the bottom of the head is almost a rectangle, with wavy triangles at the top of each side for the ears. Curve the top of the head.

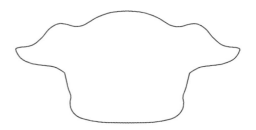

STEP 2 Add a similar smaller wavy triangular shape inside each ear. Make large oval eyes low on the face, coloring them in with black, and add arched lines over the eyes that get thinner as they go between the eyes.

STEP 3 Draw tear-shaped eyebrows above each eye and curved horns pointing inward above each eyebrow.

STEP 4 Sketch in curved lines along the length of the horns. Add an oval nose that comes to a point at the bottom, then draw a line coming down from the nose and curling up on either side.

STEP 5 Add a tuft of fur under the face that starts almost as wide as the face and curves in to a point at the center.

STEP 6 Draw Baphomet's arms next. The left arm is raised with fingers up, almost like a peace sign. Draw the right arm a little lower, with three oval fingers and a stubby thumb pointing up.

STEP 7 Sketch a large oval almost as wide as Baphomet's outstretched arms. Add curved lines to separate the crossed legs, and a hoof at the end of the legs.

STEP 8
Finally, give Baphomet some wings. Starting at the bottom of the face, draw short, diagonal lines going up, then curving down toward the hands. Add scalloped edges going down to where the legs start. Add another layer of shorter curved lines closer to the face. Add details to the eyes and color in as you like.

THE MONSTROUS

Keep going from step 1.

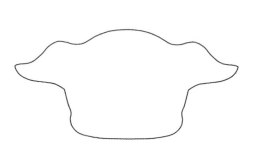

Try a few from scratch.

CERBERUS

In mythology, Cerberus is the three-headed dog that guards the gates of the underworld. Some accounts depict it with a different numbers of heads—as many as fifty!—but the three-headed version is what most people think of (and it's a lot easier to draw).

STEP 1

Sketch out the three heads. The one in the center is facing front, while the others are slightly behind the center one and turned out a bit. Give them all pointy ears that look like spades, curving the bottom of the heads and giving them straighter sides.

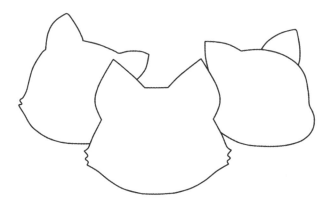

STEP 2

Add large oval eyes, two each, on the drawing's left and center heads, and one on the head on the right side of the page. Draw lines down the center of most of the ears as shown to give them depth.

STEP 3

Draw ovals over the eyes for eyebrows and ovals that come to a point at the bottom for noses. The noses sit low between the eyes. Part of the nose on the right-side face extends from the body in this view.

STEP 4

Sketch tufts of fur beneath each head. The shape across all three heads looks like a slightly curved V, with pointy edges and lines drawn in to indicate fur. Add curved lines under the noses and oval tongues on the left and center heads.

STEP 5

The heads share a body, so let's draw that next. Curve out the legs on each side to look like the sides of a heart, with a rectangular base that will become feet.

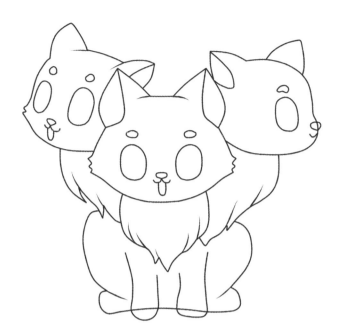

STEP 6 Draw two legs at the front and center of the body that are curved at the bottom.

STEP 7 Add a fluffy tail on the right side of the drawing, starting close to the bottom of the foot and arching up toward the face on that side.

THE MONSTROUS

STEP 8

Add details to the eyes. Erase any overlapping lines or guidelines. Color as desired.

DRAWING SPOOKY CHIBI

Practice drawing Cerberus below!

Keep going from step 1.

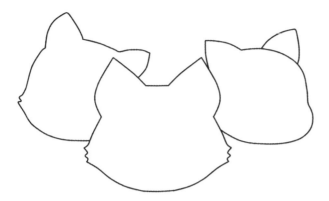

Try a few from scratch.

GOBLIN

Goblins are mischievous little creatures, and while they can look pretty scary, don't let the sweet look of this version fool you. It can still pull pranks and get into all sorts of trouble!

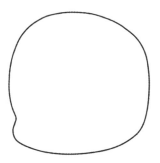

STEP 1 The goblin head is a large circle with a little divot in the goblin's lower left side.

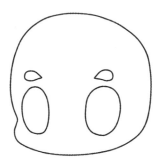

STEP 2 Add large oval eyes, with the one on the left quite close to the left side. The right eye isn't quite as far over but is spaced widely from the other eye. Add teardrop shapes for eyebrows.

STEP 3 Sketch in large triangular leaf-shaped ears and follow the shape with another set of lines inside the ears. Add lines for the inner ears. Make a nose by drawing a sideways U low between the eyes, closer to the left eye. An offset curve closer to the right eye makes a mouth, topped off with a short horizontal line.

Draw a little torso in a rough U shape.

STEP 5 Add an arm coming down from the goblin's right side, with blocky fingers closed in a fist. On the other side, draw a curve that's not overlapping the body for the arm on that side.

STEP 6 Draw long, straight, rectangular legs with rounded feet and toes.

STEP 7

Sketch shorts with zigzag edges over the legs. Add a rectangle on the left side going up to the neck and a hand with fingers gripping it. On the right side near the body, draw a circle with a smaller shape off to the side to make the goblin's cinched-up bag. We added circles to the bag, but you can decorate it however you like. Add a V shape to the center of the torso with a circle at the bottom.

STEP 8

Since our goblin doesn't have a shirt, add two dots to the chest and an X for a belly button. Add details to the eyes, erase overlapping lines or guidelines, and color as you like.

Keep going from step 1.

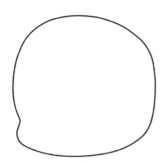

Try a few from scratch.

SWAMP MONSTER

Any mysterious place where people don't often go is sure to conjure images of spooky, scary creatures that live inside. Like Bigfoot in the deep woods, swamp monsters are a common legend in marshy areas. But also like Bigfoot, maybe these creatures are just misunderstood and really want to give you a hug.

STEP 1
Draw a large circle for the monster's head, with the top and bottom a little squared off.

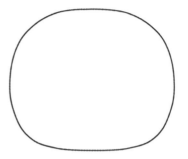

STEP 2
Add large black ovals low on the face and include dots of eyeshine.

STEP 3
Sketch a curve that's slightly longer on the swamp monster's right side, low between the eyes for its mouth. Add teardrop-shaped eyebrows above each eye.

Make two small upside-down U shapes above the mouth for nostrils. Add triangular teeth on each side of the mouth. Sketch hair that follows the line of the head, with a small indentation at the top. The hair comes to points at the front just below the bottom of the head. Add curvy triangular shapes around the face for bangs.

STEP 5 Draw wing shapes behind the head and add rectangular shapes with curved tops to give the wings depth. Add a wobbly U-shaped torso.

STEP 6 Give the swamp monster two stumpy legs pointing inward and two little outstretched arms. Our monster has four little fingers on each hand.

STEP 7 Add three teardrop-shaped toenails to each foot and squared-off claws on each finger. Draw circles in the center of each palm and smaller circles on each finger. Add a curved line to the torso.

STEP 8 Since this monster is from the swamp, sketch a wavy puddle underneath it. Add additional eye details. Erase any extra lines, and color as desired.

THE MONSTROUS

Practice drawing the swamp monster below!

Keep going from step 1.

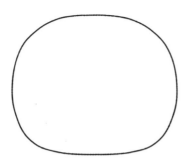

Try a few from scratch.